The

ScreenStrong

Solution

How to Free Your Child from

Addictive Screen Habits

By Melanie Hempe, BSN

For information contact:

Families Managing Media Inc.

301 E. John St.

Matthews, NC 28105

www.screenstrong.com

Cover design by Big Blue Creative

ISBN: 978-1-7325379-3-4

OTHER BOOKS
BY MELANIE HEMPE

Will Your Gamer Survive College?

Can Your Teen Survive—And Thrive—Without A Smartphone?

Available on Amazon.com

ScreenStrong™ is an initiative of Families Managing Media Inc. We provide real solutions to prevent and reverse childhood screen addictions. Using medical science as our guide, we provide a fresh approach that helps parents regain direction and confidence as they face one of today's most crucial parenting challenges: raising kids in a digital world.

Through our ScreenStrong™ programs we empower parents to take the lead and rethink cultural childhood screen trends, rebuild life skills, and reconnect families distracted by screen overuse.

For further reading on the topic of raising kids in a digital world, visit ScreenStrong.com.

For in-depth information regarding reversing the effects of electronic screen time, we recommend reading *Reset Your Child's Brain: A Four-Week Plan to End Meltdowns, Raise Grades, and Boost Social Skills by Reversing the Effects of Electronic Screen-time* by Victoria Dunckley, MD

TESTIMONIALS

"After attending your seminar, we took away the Wii and all computer games. My 8-year-old, with tears in his eyes, looked at me and whimpered, 'Don't take away the only thing I love.' When I heard that, I knew we'd made the right call.

"The time away allowed my 8-year-old to heal. He began reading. Then he read more. He tried baseball. He spent time in the woods. He started fencing. He read more. He built Legos. He started drawing. He read some more. He eventually tackled the entire *Lord of the Rings* trilogy. He is a totally reformed gamer—complete with derisive comments to anyone who talks about or plays video games in his presence. (We're working on that). One day recently he hugged me and said, 'Thanks, Mom. You saved me.' So, I want to say to you, 'Thanks. You saved my son.'"

—Mom of three boys, Charlotte, NC

"My eyes have been opened and I thank you and all those who have researched this topic. I'm so glad that we can intervene now rather than try to do it later when I'm sure it would be much harder. Since he's been off games recently, he has been playing outside constantly and more engaged with his sports. It's such a relief not to be arguing about the games and to know I'm not giving in again. Knowing how much it affects his development gives me the strength to stand firm against re-starting the cycle."

—Mom of one son, Santa Monica, CA

"Your seminar was life changing. We will never go back to the way things used to be in our home. You gave us our kids back."
—Dad of three, Boston, MA

"I took my son's phone away for a month due to poor choices he had made. After the month was over, he asked me to keep it for another month! He was really enjoying his stress-free month but was embarrassed to tell his friends that he didn't want his phone."
—Mom of one teen boy, Matthews, NC

"You saved my son. I don't know how else to explain the impact of your message at your seminar. I didn't want to leave. As you described Adam's childhood and his story, you were describing our son. It's like you were living in our house! We knew there were problems but until you gave us the words to understand them, we were lost. We have confidently removed his games. We are spending a lot of time with him as we look for new hobbies and activities. It's hard but I know in my heart that we were headed down the same path as Adam. I feel like you have saved us a lifetime of hurt and trauma. I don't know how to thank you enough for what you do. Please don't ever quit what you are doing. Families everywhere need your message."
—Mom of one boy, Fresno, CA

"All three of my teenagers have iPhones, which we regret giving to them, but seemed justifiable at the time. If I had to do it over again, we would have delayed it all together. What a big waste of time and family relationships."
—Dad of three, Orlando, FL

"Giving my daughters (now in high school) a smartphone in eighth grade was the worse parenting decision we have ever made. One of my daughters is now seeing a counselor for social media anxiety. My youngest will not get a smartphone till college. Please continue your effort to educate other parents on this message, you will save so much heartache and worse."

—Mom of three girls, Charlotte, NC

"After your seminar, I looked on my girls' phones and what I found on their phones were lies! Texting after hours, writing things they would never say in person, and even fake Instagram and Snapchat accounts. That's when we locked everything down. One of my girls had a panic attack. We had no idea that this could be addicting nor that it had become her link to a world we knew little about. If we had to do it all over again, we would have delayed the iPhone for as long as possible! We're so glad we attended your workshop and learned our intuitions were correct. Thank you!"

—Mom of two girls, Monroe, NC

"We have gone game free! Our boys are actually cooperative and are looking forward to all the new 'fun stuff' we have proposed to do instead. We are so thankful for you and your message; it has changed our lives."

—Mom of four boys, Huntersville, NC

CONTENTS

Disclaimer: This booklet will not replace the therapy or treatment center necessary to help a seriously addicted child. The information provided is not intended to constitute medical advice. Instead, all information, content, and materials are for general informational purposes only. If you feel like your child will potentially do bodily harm to you, himself or herself, you need to seek professional help. Do not use this guide as a do-it-yourself treatment program for your addicted older teen.

INTRODUCTION

"In my experience, every good parent intuitively knows what is good and not good for [their children]. The problem is, we ignore our intuitions and jump on the train loaded with mothers and fathers pushing their [children] to outshine the others. Get off of that train."
—Meg Meeker, MD, *Boys Should Be Boys: 7 Secrets to Raising Healthy Sons*

YESTERDAY, OUR KIDS WERE dressing up in princess costumes and tracking mud in the house. Today, they are standing in front of their mirrors taking selfies to build their personal brands on social media or spending hours in darkened rooms playing video games. They're lost in an adult virtual world, obsessed with video games and smartphones. As a result, kids have become more stressed, anxious, and depressed.[1] And families are being pulled apart.

How did we get here?

The addictive nature of entertainment screens has rapidly outpaced the ability of our children's brains to turn them off, let alone balance their use. Video games and social media have outsmarted parents, too. Parents are caught in the middle of a societal dilemma. We don't want our kids to be seen as outsiders because they don't have enough technology, yet we have a responsibility to protect our children from their devices. Exhausted parents are giving in. Feeling powerless, they hand over games and phones to their kids without knowing they have a choice.

Our kids are getting hurt and we must fix it. But you know that. It's why you're reading this book. It's also why you have that gut feeling that this is all too much for your kids. It's that nagging realization that 24/7 screen access, endless video game play, and constant pings and notifications aren't bringing real joy and life to your kids.

It's time to restore balance in your home.

It's time to pry your gamer off the sofa so he can get his driver's license, go fishing with his dad, or just make eye contact during a conversation. It's time that your daughter seeks advice from you instead of her 300 Instagram followers. It's time to restore these relationships.

All you need are some facts and clear direction.

I have been exactly where you are, at the end of my rope raising a gamer son. After making some uninformed, unfortunate choices with him, I began to search for answers. Thankfully, I found answers in brain science and years of research.

I discovered that video games and social media are not necessary for healthy child development. They are highly addictive and harmful to many kids. And though our screen-obsessed culture may seem like the new normal, we don't have to accept it as the only option. Just because something is common does not mean it's normal.

That's why we developed ScreenStrong™. A ScreenStrong lifestyle is about keeping the benefits and delaying the harm of technology. Practically, this means that you hit the pause button on your children's recreational screens—video games, social media, and smartphones—until they are ready to handle the responsibility. And it's much easier than you think.

THE BIG QUESTION

Let me ask you a question: are screens, video games, and social media bringing you and your family joy?

If you answered yes, then you can close this book because you don't need what comes next. But, if you answered no, then it's time to fix things.

Your child might try to tell you his screens bring joy, but his meltdowns, drama, and unsafe practices tell you otherwise. If screens are not enriching your family, then you need to make a change.

Here is what I recommend you do so that your family can stop being held victim by the digital world and start living ScreenStrong: *delay the devices.*

I'm not suggesting you remove all screens from your home. I'm talking about the addictive video games and small screens in your children's pockets that trap them and get them into trouble. It's okay to delay. It's okay to pause screen use until your kids can handle it with more maturity. Our recommendation is to delay through late adolescence. Read that statement again. *It's okay to delay.*

The first step to freeing your child from screen dependency is to understand that delaying is a great option. The second step is to stop believing the cultural myth that all kids must grow up with recreational screen entertainment.[2]

COMMON MISCONCEPTIONS

If I take my child's screen away, he will hate me.
Don't believe that your kids will hate you for replacing their screen time with strong family connections and real-life fun. Initially, you may be met with resistance, but deep down they want and need more real connection with family and friends.

My child won't have any friends if I take away her screens.
Don't believe that she will lose all her friends. In reality, she will gain the opportunity to make more friends because she will be participating in a variety of activities, thus expanding her world. I'm referring to face-to-face, real-life friendships, not more followers on social media. Screen-free time together develops more personal and deeper relationships. Ultimately that's what our kids crave.

My child will be left out without social media.

Our experience shows that kids feel more left out on social media than they do when they are off it. Science backs this up. The peak year for social rejection is the age of 15 for girls.[3] Fifteen is also the watershed year for defining one's in-group. When you understand that your child will be potentially hurt more on social media between eighth and 11th grade than any other time in her life, you may reconsider that smartphone.[4,5] This early trauma is hard to overcome, and spending more time on social media can make it worse.

All kids need smartphones and social media.

What's the best age for a smartphone? The short answer is when you trust that your child will be mature enough to avoid distractions and temptations—and porn. From what we know about brain science and the age of maturity, delaying is a good option. There is a big risk with early use, but no risk in delaying. If a phone is a must, internet and data-free phones work fine for when practice is cancelled.[6]

My son will become a famous YouTuber/Gamer.

Don't believe that your son will become a rich and famous video gamer because he told you about some guy somewhere who did. He probably has a better chance of winning the lottery than he does at becoming the next eSports all-star. There are currently more than 200 million registered users of *Fortnite* alone. Is it worth it for him to play for eight hours a day? Is that how you want him to spend his only childhood? Don't let an exception to the rule or the quest for fame become the reason your child drops out of your family.

If I delay, she will binge on screens when she gets to college.
Don't believe that kids who have a low-tech lifestyle, like many
tech executives' kids,[7] will grow up and binge on tech in college.[8]
Your child will bring the interests and hobbies to college that he
built in childhood. If screens are his main hobby, then he will
likely bring his screen hobby to college, because little gamers
grow up to be big gamers. Leonard Sax, author of *The Collapse of
Parenting*, says it well: "There are no guarantees. But the research
strongly suggests that if you inspire habits of good behavior and
self-control in your son or daughter throughout childhood and
adolescence, then you have improved the odds that your child
will continue to do the right thing after leaving home."[9]

Technology is the future; my child won't be prepared.
Kids don't use screens the way adults do. They don't learn
technology skills by playing video games or spending hours on
social media. They are exposed to plenty of screens in our day
to day lives without having their own. You are doing just fine on
your screens today, and you didn't sleep with them or grow up
with them in your pocket. Screen technology is designed to be
easy enough for a 3-year-old—an age where he can't tie his own
shoes but has the capability to use a smartphone. Your child
does not need years of training on *World of Warcraft* or *Candy
Crush* to be prepared for a job down the road.

All kids these days have screens, so mine need them too.
You have a choice. Recreational screens are *not required* for a
healthy and normal childhood. It may feel like everyone plays
video games and has a smartphone, but many kids don't, and
that number is growing. Our culture will continue to push new

tech on kids. But after reviewing the research, and their children's emotional health, parents are reconsidering.

Your child will have a better chance to use screens in a balanced, productive way when he has had time to develop adequate self-control and judgment.

Unfortunately, I learned this the hard way.

OUR STORY

My oldest son, Adam, became addicted to video games on my watch and with my permission.

Looking back, I can easily see the warning signs and spot exactly how it happened. I can piece together the many wrong turns that we took during those years in middle and high school that seemed so innocent at the time. I had plenty of excuses mixed in with a few myths:

He had good grades.
He needed and deserved "downtime" on his game.
His computer use was making him smart.
He was learning to code.
His gaming friends were his only friends.
He wasn't getting in trouble.

Ultimately, I wanted him to be happy. Like every other mom out there, I would do just about anything to make that possible. I wanted him to love me. I was emotionally invested in his game as much as he was. After all, it was just a game, so how harmful could it be? But I didn't recognize the warning signs. We were not prepared for what unfolded during his teen years as he disappeared further into his gaming. The stress. The conflicts. The broken connection with him. The lost childhood. Our family was caught off guard.

Thankfully, Adam's story ends well. But only after he dropped out of college due to excessive gaming and not finishing classes. He served for five years in the military, where he learned valuable life skills, and finally returned to college and got back on track.[10]

After living with the beast of screen addiction, we delayed smartphone and social media access until late adolescence for our younger children and shifted to a video game-free home.[11]

I'm happy to say all our kids are still alive, they're not social outcasts, and they're happy as clams.

They get plenty of screen experiences when they use technology as the helpful tool it was designed to be. But we don't allow the highly addictive devices in their pockets or as part of their daily routines. We have successfully removed the screen drama and have maintained screen balance by giving them age-appropriate use without the risk of addiction. We discovered the secret. Our family is more connected than we were before, and we've never looked back!

But honestly, it's not a secret. It may seem countercultural, but it's no secret. Once again, the key phrase is: *it's okay to delay*. If you're ready to make a change and reverse even the slightest hint of screen dependency that your child may be experiencing, then it's time to take action. This book will help you. The process will take work on your end and retraining on his end. It may include a few tantrums and meltdowns. But the time and effort are worth the payoff.

The steps in this guide will help you find your way out of the darkened rooms and virtual worlds, and back to a balanced, healthy family life. These steps are based on many years of research, my relationships with doctors dedicated to the study of childhood screen addictions, and my daily experience of raising four children currently in middle school through college.

But perhaps even more influential are the recommendations based on my experiences with hundreds of families just like yours who have come to our life-changing workshops. They've learned to power down the screens and power up real-life experiences. Just like they did, you can learn how to reduce screen conflicts in your home and reclaim your kids.

Are you ready to rethink screens, reclaim your kids, and reconnect your family? Let's go rescue your kids! We will begin by reviewing what science tells us about their brains.

THE
BRAIN SCIENCE

*"What you do and learn in life physically changes what your brain looks like—
it literally rewires it."*

—John Medina, PhD, *Brain Rules: 12 Principles for Surviving and
Thriving at Work, Home, and School*

HAVE YOU EVER WITNESSED the screen coma look on your
child's face? When you've seen that look, you've probably felt in
your gut that something wasn't right. That built-in parent alarm
system is telling you that it's time for a change. You instinctively
know that the process of growing up, like most everything else
in nature, has a cycle and a season. When this order is
interrupted, the developmental process breaks down, changing
the trajectory of a child's life.

Screens can disrupt the ever-so-important brain development
process. Let's take a moment to consider a few facts about brain
development to reinforce the fact that it's okay to hit that pause
button on your kid's screens.

BRAIN DEVELOPMENT

Teen brains are under construction.

Our kids don't use screens like we do because they are not mature enough yet. In fact, it takes about 25 years for the executive function area in the brain—the frontal cortex—to mature.[1] I remember thinking that Adam was an adult when he was 16 because he was shaving and was taller than I was. I thought I was done with much of my parenting. How wrong I was.

The emotional center of the brain develops before the thinking part of the brain. This explains the rollercoaster behavior of up one minute, down the next. Teens are skilled at acceleration, but terrible at pumping the brakes when things start spinning out of control. They aren't quite ready for the distractions and temptations of excessive screen entertainment. Their stimulation-seeking brains love novelty, which is why they are so enthralled by interactive video games and phones. They will bypass common sense and head straight for risky behavior on social media. It's also why they need parents—and our fully developed frontal cortex.

Regardless of your child's IQ or your sharp parenting skills, it's impossible to accelerate the maturation process. There is no shortcut for teaching wisdom, either; that develops slowly over time and takes an abundance of life experience. So relax and enjoy this stage because you can't speed it up.

Activities shape the brain.

Your child's brain is custom-tailored to match his environment and activities. Specific areas of the brain are developed based on exposure to certain experiences. Childhoods dominated by screen use can produce lopsided brains.[2] Critical pathways do not get enough attention, while the reward center receives too much.

Puberty fine-tunes the brain.

Puberty marks the beginning of a complex demolition and rebuilding process in your child's brain. This simply means that in an effort for the brain to work efficiently, frequently used neuronal connections are strengthened and others are pruned away.[3] For example, the ability to learn music and languages is easier when we are younger. Our goal is to help our children have many varied experiences, developing as much of the brain as possible during this window of rich potential. Our kids' brains are in a race against time, so don't let them waste too much of it on a mindless screen.

HOW TO BUILD A STRONG BRAIN

Here are a few of the many components necessary to help your child build a balanced, healthy brain:

Connection with humans: touch, conversation, and empathy
Belonging—to be connected to other people in a family and community—is the most important need every person has. When face-to-face relationships are built and nurtured the brain, our social organ, benefits most.[4] Human touch and meaningful conversation are part of this formula along with

unconditional love and empathy best delivered by parents. Children need a strong sense of acceptance and love to stay healthy.

The real work of creating and building relationships must be done in person before being transferred over to a screen. While screen connections are convenient, ultimately, they will not meet the need for belonging, especially for a child or teen. The isolating nature of screen use can also promote loneliness, which is harmful to developing brains. This can then easily lead to increased stress, anxiety, and depression.

Movement and real play

Optimal brain development requires physical movement and exercise in order to bring plenty of oxygen to the brain. No amount of swiping a screen will fire new connections the way physical activity will. Now a proven treatment for learning and attention problems, physical movement builds the brain and helps regulate excess energy.[5] Healthy movement also enhances learning. But every minute a child spends on a screen is a minute he's not moving. He isn't engaging in real play on a screen either. Physical play is never found on a screen. Imaginative and unstructured play is most beneficial when done using multiple senses.[6]

Sleep and downtime

During sleep, the brain goes to work, organizing things from the day and cleaning things up. Teenagers need over nine hours of sleep—more sleep than their parents need. But kids are not getting enough sleep partly due to poor screen habits.[7]

Video games and social media stimulate the adrenal glands and raise cortisol levels. When cortisol is raised, melatonin, the hormone necessary for sleep, is suppressed. With a lack of sleep comes more isolation and less critical thinking. With less sleep, your teen will have a limited perspective on reality because her guard is down.

"Sleep isn't a luxury," writes Dr. Frances Jensen, MD, in her book *The Teenage Brain: A Neuroscientist's Survival Guide to Raising Adolescents and Young Adults.* "Memory and learning are thought to be consolidated during sleep, so it's a requirement for adolescents and as vital to their health as the air they breathe and the food they eat. In fact, sleep helps them eat better. It also helps them manage stress."[8]

KIDS' BRAINS ON SCREENS

Screen use is not the benign activity we once thought it was; however, not all screens are created equal. For example, television viewing has a different effect on a developing brain than using screens to play video games or explore with social media. Interactive screens involve a high level of brain stimulation. This kind of screen use has the penitential to do the most damage during the pre-adulthood years.

Excessive gaming and social media use can affect the brain in the following ways:

Cause a chemical dependency
Much like drugs or alcohol, interactive screen activity stimulates the reward and pleasure center of the brain by releasing a mix of

neurochemicals, including the feel-good chemical, dopamine. Oxytocin is also released, causing your child to bond and fall in love with her device. A craving cycle develops. As screen use increases over time, so does the craving. Discovering this fact was a game changer for me. I had no idea that brain chemicals were involved. As it turns out, my kids weren't deliberately ignoring me, they were drugged.[9] One day Adam told me, "That game did something to me." I know now that he wasn't shifting blame; he was correct.

Cause a real addiction

The dopamine addiction reward cycle is the villain in our story, not the screens themselves. Novelty (new photos, notifications, etc.) and new content (new game levels, rewards, etc.) produce the highest dopamine payout because the brain interprets new information as a reward. Your child's smartphone and game console are low-effort novelty machines. The brain quickly learns and remembers where all that dopamine is coming from, orienting itself to want more. Your child can get a good feeling just looking at her phone. Just hearing the familiar video game theme song or seeing the gaming console can trigger your son to want to play. When the brain is more excited about screen rewards and less excited about everyday life, your child is in trouble.[10]

Trigger physical stress

Screen use causes the fight/flight center—the amygdala—to be stimulated. This effect is so strong that the logical part of the brain—the frontal cortex—begins to shut down, making it hard for your child to think clearly about a situation.[11,12] This triggers adrenaline, which leads to increased heart rate, blood pressure, and the stress hormone cortisol. It can also be accompanied by a decrease in blood sugar and difficulties sleeping. Over time, the body struggles to return to a normal state, resulting in chronic stress. This feeling of being under low levels (and sometime high levels) of chronic stress is harmful for a developing brain and leads to further physical and mental problems, including anxiety and depression.[13]

Incite extreme behaviors

The emotional toll felt by your child is a direct effect of the physical responses mentioned above. It's difficult for a teen to constantly manage her personal brand on social media. The daily cascade of stress, over-stimulation, and immediate screen gratification leads to extreme behaviors. In your home this may surface as meltdowns, tantrums, and disrespect. You may even see your teen throwing emotional fits like a toddler which may be why you're reading this guide.

You can become afraid of your child and exhausted over the fight to get him or her off the device. This is not the recipe for a healthy childhood.[14] Behaviors such as bullying, sexting, cheating in school, and engaging in social media gossip are the cause of much of the stress, anxiety, and depression that are so common in our teens' digital worlds.

Introduce distractions

Millions of dollars are spent to keep young brains attached to the closest screen. Your children may have high IQs, but they will never outsmart the psychological pull of the screen. They are distracted while they are on the screen, and they are also distracted by their screens when they are off them. Just the promise of engaging with screens after chores or homework will keep your child from focusing on their current task, and even encourage them to rush through the process. Your teen craves low-effort, high-reward activities. Moving back and forth between the mindless virtual world and the harder real world is exhausting. This is why many parents feel that their teens are stuck in immaturity. Teens are not moving toward the harder work of becoming independent and growing up.

SCREEN ADDICTION

"The 15-year-old brain is not the same as a 30-year-old brain, and so things are not going to affect it the same. And that's true of alcohol and it's also true of violent video games."
—David Walsh, PhD, *Why Do They Act that Way? A Survival Guide to the Adolescent Brain for You and Your Teen*

It's not easy to look at our kids and think they are addicted to something. But medical research is pointing to the serious nature of screen obsession in childhood and adolescence (see *Appendix 2*). Now that we understand that screen use can be addictive, we are able to fix the problem.

A screen addiction is an online compulsive behavior that dominates your child's life. This behavior pattern interferes with normal living to the extent that it takes priority over other activities and interests and causes severe stress on the child and on family and friends. This pattern continues to escalate despite negative consequences.

Reviewing best practices around other addictions helps us prevent screen addiction. With a potentially addictive behavior, exposure at younger ages adds to the risk of developing an addiction. This is because the young brain is very malleable, undergoing a complex developmental process, with some areas maturing sooner than others. Knowing that screen use follows the same patterns as other potentially addictive behavior, we should:

- *Minimize early exposure.* Don't allow your children and teens develop an early dependency on their screens.
- *Maximize relationships.* Change the environment to reflect a people-centered, not screen-centered, lifestyle.

Before we go any further, it's important to take a moment to assess your child's screen use.[15] Here is a general list of warning signs to determine if your child is at risk for screen dependency. If you observe one or more of the following warning signs in your child, you may need to rethink your current plan:

- ☐ Only screen use puts your child in a good mood.
- ☐ Child is unhappy when forced to unplug.
- ☐ Screen use is increasing over time.
- ☐ Child uses screen time as an escape.
- ☐ Screens are the only reward that motivate the child.
- ☐ Child sneaks around & lies about screen use.
- ☐ Child has a general increase in anxiety and stress.
- ☐ Screens interfere with family activities, friendships, or school.

FROM A FORMER GAMER

The gamer's world is the virtual world, and the real world is just a nuisance that pulls him away from his reality. Everything is about the game. Everything he does in the real world is done in order to get back to the gaming world as quickly as possible. His thoughts are always on the game and how to improve or what to do next.

A gamer always talks about the game. Instead of making an intentional decision to take time out of his day to play, his natural state is finding comfort in playing video games. The truth is, he must pull himself away from the game in order to do life in the real world. The limbic system in his brain can't distinguish between what's real and what's fake which is why visualization is such a powerful tool. The subconscious mind believes that visualizations are real. Even remembering a scary event from the past can initiate the release of adrenaline.

When the gamer progresses in the game, his subconscious believes that he's progressing in real life. It associates the game with the good feeling you get from making progress in anything. But you can't make meaningful progress with anything in the real world in 10 minutes like you can in a video game. Most accomplishments in life take lots of time, energy, practice, and grit. This causes the gamer to lose interest in real-world activities because nothing can measure up to the pace of video games. His brain has literally been wired to think that his success and productivity lie with the video games, and that everything else is a waste of time because it isn't as efficient.

In the following chapters, I lay out seven steps that will help you free your child from screen dependency and set you on the path for delaying access, so you can reclaim your kids and reconnect as a family.

(To find out where your child falls on the gaming level scale, go to page 89.)

STEP ONE:
BECOME A COACH

"The traditional family hierarchy has been turned on its head. Our culture has marginalized parents and teachers as technologically incompetent and maintains that kids are better judges of how they should use their devices and time."

—Richard Freed, PhD, *Wired Child*

LIKE AN UNWELCOME PLAYER on your team, screens have invaded your home and have undermined your role as leader. This power struggle started during the younger years when your child's screen was disguised as a wonderful babysitter. Slowly the screen started becoming a substitute parent for your child. Now, your child demands screen stimulation and depends on the screen instead of you for most of his emotional and relationship needs. He has lost respect for you, and your authority is being tested daily.

Every team needs a strong leader, and parents—not kids—are best suited for this job. Think of your role as not just a parent, but as a coach. It's time to rework the game plan, go back to the locker room, make some changes, and give an inspiring pep talk to your players. Turning this season around may be difficult, but it's not impossible!

ADOPT A COACH'S MENTALITY

Take a minute to recall your childhood team sports experiences. Now think about your favorite coach and the role he played in your life. More than likely your coach was not your best friend. He was strict and taught you about discipline and hard work. You are probably smiling right now as you think of how he pushed you past your comfort zone in order to help you reach your potential. But you are also smiling because your coach had your back and you were a better person for knowing him.

Many people can trace their adult successes to these types of relationships from childhood: adults who cared deeply, taught them work ethic and discipline, and pushed them to reach high goals. Whether or not you agreed with all their methods, deep down you knew they had your best interests at heart.

Now take that perspective and apply it to your parenting. You care deeply about the real success of your children—your team—and their ability to work with others in the real world. That ability will affect their jobs, roommates, future spouses, and families. You care about developing them individually. You also have a clear vision for the direction of your team, and you will do the hard work to make it successful.

But your team is experiencing a losing season right now.

So do what a good coach does. Go back to the fundamentals, do the research, and rework the game plan. Focus on the role you have as a coach. Admit that mistakes have been made along this journey with your children. Even if screen time started with good intentions, it took your team to places you never predicted. Now you're saying, "No more!" "Not in this house!" You are stepping up as the coach that your team members need right now to get them refocused and moving in a healthy direction.

DEVELOP YOUR GAME PLAN

Your children desperately need adults to guide them. Even your older teens still need boundaries. Your game plan should start with pushing the pause button on the wasteful and harmful influence of screens until your child is mature enough to handle them.

Teens with warm, caring parents who set high standards and maintain a high level of discipline and boundaries (see diagram of parenting styles) do better in life than kids with uninvolved or overly permissive parents.

In her book, *Grit: The Power of Passion and Perseverance*, psychologist Angela Duckworth, PhD, says of authoritative (or wise) parents, "They appreciate that children need love, limits, and latitude to reach their full potential. Their authority is based on knowledge and wisdom rather than power...teens with warm, respectful, and demanding parents earned higher grades in school, were more self-reliant, suffered less from anxiety and depression, and were less likely to display delinquent behavior."[1]

In other words, when parents combine their own wisdom with loving care for their kids, they increase the chances of success all the way around.

A ScreenStrong Family seeks to apply the authoritative parenting approach to the management of screen use in their homes. This game plan ultimately seeks to bring about the following outcomes for your team (i.e. your family):

- Less stress and anxiety in your home.
- Fewer arguments and conflict over screen use.
- More communication with your child.
- Screen-free meals (at home and out) together.
- More focus on other hobbies, school, and life skills.
- More family time together.
- More success at school and extracurricular activities.
- More physical activity.

I'm sure you can think of some other goals for your family.

Having a game plan is a critical first step. Even if you understand your role as a coach and have a great game plan, you'll need the right support and preparation for that game plan to succeed. Step 2 will describe how you start to gather that support.

DIAGRAM OF PARENTING STYLES

Research points to the authoritative parenting style with a high degree of warmth and a high degree of control as the most beneficial for long term success.[2]

TIP: Limit your non-work screen activity in front of your kids as well. You will need to be more available and present, especially in the beginning. Remember, they are watching you and what you value. Be sure to tell them why this is important to you, and how it supports your family values. In turn, these reminders will only enhance their family attachment as they will identify with what makes your family unique and special, and feel validated as an important link in your family unit.

STEP TWO: GATHER SUPPORT

"Improving and revising our kids' screen plan is so much easier when you get your friends to join in with you; in fact, it's almost impossible without their support."
    —Jen, Mom of three, ScreenStrong workshop attendee

EVERY COACH KNOWS THAT assistants are needed to run a winning team. So it's time to assemble your support team.

WHY SUPPORT MATTERS

Helping your child kick the screen habit is hard work. Be prepared for pushback and resistance. Here are some potholes you're likely to encounter in the road ahead. You'll need a solid support system to avoid being derailed by them.

Resistance

Don't be surprised or upset when your tween says that she hates you or that no one in the whole world is as mean as you. You are taking her drug away, and it feels unnatural and uncomfortable.

A few hard weeks

Depending on the level of screen immersion your child is used to, there will be an inevitable physical letdown when you dial it back. Your child's body became accustomed to a higher, unnatural level of dopamine caused by screen overuse. The changes you are making are likely to cause some feelings of withdrawal and/or depression. It will take some time to unwind and reset; he needs your help. Don't lose hope. This is temporary.

Regression

The screen addicted child may regress emotionally to the age when he became most addicted. This happens with other addictions as well. If he started checking out of life in middle school and turned to gaming to avoid the natural awkwardness of social development, he will still have to do this developmental work. He may panic. He doesn't know how to fill the void with real life because he has not been practicing that. Removing screens will expose the skills never developed, such as initiating friendships, planning social events, making eye contact in conversations, and resolving peer conflicts. These skills still need to be learned or relearned.

Aggression

Severely addicted older teens may become especially aggressive, make threats, throw or kick things, call you names, or even hit you. Take these outbursts seriously and call 911 if the situation escalates and you feel threatened. It's important to let your teen know ahead of time that you will call 911 if he gets out of control.

Frustration toward your child

Many parents secretly feel that they don't like their screen-addicted children anymore. Of course, you love your child, but screen-addicted people can be difficult to be around. Chances are that you have been feeling a resentment toward your child for several years, and you are at the end of your rope. Although you may feel tempted, do not take your frustration out on your child. Take full responsibility for the screen dependency in your child's life. He did not buy the screens and allow them. You did. Be calm, be upbeat, and don't get upset. Look ahead instead.

Your own doubt

We want our kids to be happy. We can hardly stand the thought of them being upset. That's why it's so important to have a support system. You will have weak moments when you think you can lock down the phone and limit the game. Resist the urge to give in. A coach must stand strong.

Trust that these potholes in the road will get smaller or even disappear entirely over time. You are taking positive steps to get it back in balance now. The community that you form is key to your success.

Call and talk with a like-minded friend, educate yourself more about the issue, and start a ScreenStrong small group.[1] Stay strong and steady in front of your child.

RECRUIT YOUR ASSISTANT COACHES

SPOUSE

The first and most impactful action in building support is to get your spouse (or significant other) in sync with the plan. If that's not possible because your spouse is a gamer or you are a single parent, it's especially important to get a support system of friends or other family members in place right away.

FRIENDS AND FAMILY MEMBERS

Contact your extended local family members and let them know the plan. Next, contact the parents of your child's close friends and ask for their support and encouragement. Let them know that you still want their child to socialize with your child, but without video games and smartphones. Encourage these parents to support your plan when your child is in their households. For teens, you will want to make a list of their friends, so you can help them organize and plan social activities. It's better to have kids at your house as much as possible as you begin to make these major changes. If you focus only on the screen changes at your house, your child will just live at his friends' houses so he can game or use social media. We suggest planning in-person social activities at least once a week until your teen takes the lead. And don't let your kids (or even older teens) hang out at friends' house without an adult present if possible.

CAREGIVERS

Inform other adult caretakers (nanny, babysitter, grandparents, etc.) of the new family screen plan. Spell out what that means for the time the children will be in their care. Explain the reasons why this is important. Like you, they care about the health and well-being of your child. The same rules should apply no matter who is caring for your child.

TEACHERS AND COACHES

Next to parents, teachers are the most influential people in a child's life. Let's get them on your team early. As he gets older your child will generally need to access school computers during school hours, so it's crucial to discuss the use of laptops/tablets and phones at school with the administration. Let them know that your child is struggling with screen overuse. If there are other means of class communication via group text or apps, make sure teachers have your phone number to direct their communications to your phone. For many reasons, adults should not be privately texting your children. It's a much better practice for them to email your child and copy you on the email. Your school should accommodate your position regarding your child's screen use. If it helps, explain it the way you would explain a peanut allergy. Accommodations must be made.[2]

START A SCREENSTRONG SMALL GROUP

This is easy to do. Identify a few other families that are willing to partner with you to start a ScreenStrong small group, which often begins as a book club. When you join with a few like-minded families to get more informed, share activities, outings and ideas, everyone benefits. The increased accountability and encouragement are a life saver. Many people are looking for solutions to screen conflicts and, like you, want to make new low-tech friends. Invite parents from your school, neighborhood, or church to learn more about preventing and reducing screen addictions. As you are getting your group together, begin reading a recommended book on your own. Try our book list to get started.[3]

TIP: When you meet resistance from your child, enlist the help of a well-respected, like-minded family member, friend, or even a coach to help with the discussion. There is such a great benefit to having other adult voices in your child's adolescent journey. Work together, so he knows how to jump in and help. Your child's community needs to know what's happening, especially when he's older, and his community is larger.

STEP THREE: PREPARE FOR CHANGE

"When a habit emerges, the brain stops fully participating in decision making. It stops working so hard, or diverts focus to other tasks. So unless you deliberately fight a habit—unless you find new routines—the pattern will unfold automatically."

—Charles Duhigg, *The Power of Habit*

ALTHOUGH IT MAY FEEL like it, your child's screen habits were not created overnight. They were formed over time in the nooks and crannies of his daily routine. The habit started off slowly and grew as it replaced other activities. So unwinding it will take preparation on your end. Your success will depend on how well you prepare for change.

CHANGE YOUR ROUTINES

When we associate satisfaction and rewards with a routine, a craving emerges in our brain that drives the habit loop and can lead to an addiction.[1] When kids establish unhealthy routines surrounding screen use, we must intervene to change those routines. Here are some typical times in many family routines when screen time is a challenge:

- o Right after school.
- o Immediately after dinner.
- o During homework.
- o Before bed.
- o Whenever they normally get tired or hungry.

Here are some ways to alter your routines to address these challenging times:

- ❖ Implement a no-screens rule in the car. Talk and listen to music instead.
- ❖ Don't drive straight home after school. Go by a park or meet friends out for frozen yogurt first.
- ❖ Before kids come home from school, put out healthy snacks for them to enjoy when they walk in the door. Join the kids and talk about their day or have a snack in the car when you pick them up.
- ❖ Increase face-to-face social time with friends. Plan for friends to come over after school if they live nearby. Encourage your kids to call their friends at night and talk on the phone. (See Tip at the end of this chapter.)
- ❖ Sit with them while they do homework and get screen homework done right away, hopefully before dinner, or in the kitchen while you are doing dishes.
- ❖ Go on a mandatory family walk after dinner.

- ❖ Be present and plan traditions like pizza and family game night on Fridays or Saturdays.
- ❖ Establish family rituals right before bed. Read together as a family instead of everyone retreating to their own screen corners.

Over time, healthier patterns will be strengthened, and your child will settle into habits that don't involve devices. The mom of an elementary-age boy recalls, "When we pulled the game out of our house, he would go outside after dinner and throw the baseball against the house and catch it over and over. He made the team that spring and I think that the repetition really helped!"

If your daughter gets on her social media for hours right after school, change that routine and plan another activity during that time. One mom did this by taking her daughter to get a snack and meet up with a friend after school at a coffee shop. Another group of moms with younger kids planned a stop by the nearby park to let the kids run around and get some energy out before they got home. Get creative. Meet a friend at the local library to get homework done. If there is a playground at school, meet there after school. This gives the kids a chance to play together and the parents a chance to visit. It takes planning and time, but it's worth it. And the kids love it.

Your job is to step back and recognize the routines, then plan to change them as needed. Your child will not be able to focus on new rewards if the screen is always lurking in the same nooks and crannies of your routine every day.

RESET YOUR HOME

Your child's environment directly affects how time is spent at home. If devices are in every room, he will be hard pressed not to gravitate toward them. And if your child has become accustomed to spending her time on a device when she's in your home, then we must reset your home to retrain her habits.

When it comes to battling addiction, environment matters a lot. Many people go through rehab only to return home and struggle with the same temptations that got them in trouble in the first place. When we create a fresh environment for our kids, we will increase their chance for success during the process of restoring healthy habits. This may even require looking at which friends' homes are good environments for supporting the changes you are making.

Your child's screen environment is your home. When you walk in the front door, how many screens are calling your child's name? Take a screen inventory. What's in the den? On the kitchen table? In his bedroom? Many homes have game controllers and wires hanging from the big TV in the den. How is your child going to get a needed break when every room has controllers, remotes, or tablets everywhere?

Begin to think of ways to make your home more calm, peaceful, fun, and less screen-centric. The goal is to increase the opportunities for family connections, to lower the stress level, and to just enjoy being physically present with one another.

Purposefully setting a positive, fresh, new tone in your home will make a big difference in interrupting old patterns. The objective is to create a warm and welcoming environment not just for your family, but for your kids and their friends—one in which they will want to hang out and engage.

Here are some ways to change the atmosphere of your home:

- **Sounds.** Keep a music channel on the TV during the day. Enjoy music together; ditch the earbuds.
- **Smells.** Bake bread or light scented candles to conjure warm emotions.
- **Tastes.** Put healthy snacks out during transition times to take advantage of their power to set a warm, loving tone in your home.
- **Fun.** Keep games and puzzles out in easy view. And don't forget outside: tree swings, trampolines, ping pong tables, and basketball hoops are always a hit.

It may be helpful to gather some supplies ahead of time. Think through what you may need: an alarm clock for their bedroom, a watch, new books and a book light, basketball hoop over the bedroom door, craft supplies and kids' magazines, to name a few items.

RESET BEYOND THE HOME FRONT

Be sure to consider more than what happens between your home's four walls daily. Make sure you're prepared for the following situations:

Car rides and wait times

Have books on tape, conversation-cards, travel art/drawing supplies, travel games, and snacks and water on hand. Limit in-car movie entertainment to long trips. Car rides and wait times are invaluable talk times or even quiet times to reflect and process the day. Don't let devices steal those precious moments. For older teens, it may be the best time to get them to talk with you about school and life.

Playdates and get togethers

If we're calling it a play date, then let's make sure they can actually play together in real life. Have board games, crafts, and outdoor toys (balls, Slip 'N Slide, sprinklers, bikes, etc.). For older kids: bike to get ice cream, play cul-de-sac football and driveway basketball, play Wiffle Ball, and throw a Frisbee. The list is long.

Sleepovers

Put a hold on sleepovers for now. Let your child still attend the party but pick her up at 9:30-10:00 p.m. We call these half-overs. There is no way you can control what other people do in their homes and your child will likely find a screen. We introduced this in our community and now it's common to have half-overs. Nothing good happens after 10:00 p.m. anyway! A good coach knows what their players are doing on and off the field.

Family friends

Be intentional about the influence of other adults in your child's life. Your village is not just immediate family. Invite old and new friends over to enjoy non-screen time together. Look back at Step 2 and review your support system. Find a few like-minded friends to invite over. Part of the fun of this new lifestyle is rekindling and developing new friendships. Make potluck dinners part of your new ScreenStrong small group tradition.

Don't miss the importance of preparing for change. Helping your child change her screen habit will be much easier now that you have taken the time to look at how your routines and your environment can impact that habit.

TIP: We use our cordless phone system as our home phone. It's connected to our cellular network. So our kids can call their friends or us when they are home, but they don't have a smartphone. They can even plug this in at another home if they have a need to do that (i.e. babysitting). Many families have success with a basic phone that acts as the home phone and stays in the kitchen.

TIP: Repaint or rearrange your child's room. Let him do it with you. That should keep him busy for a while! Let him decorate it with posters, his artwork, or pick out new bedding. Create a cozy reading nook. Frame some photos and suggest he even decorate his door. One mom made a photo collage of all of her daughter's friends and put them over her bed to replace her Instagram account.

STEP FOUR: REMOVE THE SCREENS

"Nearly all children will have a negative emotional or behavioral reaction when they hear their beloved devices will be gone, but know if other parents have survived it, you can too."

—Victoria Dunckley, MD, *Reset Your Child's Brain*

OKAY, COACH. IT'S TIME to gather your players and lay out the game plan. I'm going to be honest; this is a tough step. The younger the kids, the easier it will be. During this conversation, you will explain that you have learned some things about brain development, you are taking the blame, the family will be taking a screen break, they will spend more time with their friends in person, and you will be having more fun together as a family.

TALK WITH YOUR KIDS

Chances are, if your child has been overusing his screens, he may think he's in charge. But he's not, and this isn't a debate.

You're the coach and you're announcing the new game plan. You're not asking your team for a lot of feedback right now. Your attitude is more important than your child's attitude at this point. Using a positive, upbeat tone and direct but light-hearted communication is your goal. You are not mad. You are confident in your direction. Your past screen-time conversations have turned into arguments but this one won't. The way you present the news will set the stage for success. Think about how an inspiring coach would present it. "We've had a rough season and we must make adjustments." Don't have a sad or upset look on your face. Smile, be happy, and get excited about spending more time with your kids. They will follow your lead—eventually!

Plan for the conversation to occur right before an already scheduled family weekend away from home if possible. If you can't get away, plan a weekend of non-tech activities. Tell then that you are taking a break from video games and smartphones. Give them an overview of the dangers of screen overuse, how it affects their brains, and how it becomes a habit. Keep it simple. Don't apologize and don't overexplain. Visit our website for simple science information that you can use. Bringing in the science will help the conversation not get too personal. Let them know that you are taking full responsibility for the current situation; it's not their fault and it's also not the end of the world.

Depending on the age of your children, you will need to determine the level of communication. For younger kids, keep in mind that they are not mature enough to understand all the reasons. Nor do you need to fully make the case. After all, they don't understand why they can't have a bowl of candy and a soft drink for dinner either.

With older teens, be confident, loving, and supportive, but firm. Be more conversational, but remember, there is *no negotiating*. Coaches know what's best for their team and they lead. Ultimately, your children will be more at peace knowing you are in charge. You must trust that your role as their coach is internally helping them feel more at ease and secure.

PREPARE FOR THE RESPONSE

Be prepared for pushback, including organized and thought-out pushback. One mom called me stunned after her initial conversation with her middle-school daughter about why they were going to continue to delay the smartphone. Her daughter decided it was time to do some research of her own in an effort to win her parents over. She came with a typed report on why she needed a smartphone. This is so common that I have named these exercises *The Middle-School-Girl Smartphone Speech*. It was researched, had references, and was well thought through from her perspective. "My husband thought surely she deserves the right to get a smartphone because it was such an impressive piece of literature," the mom said. "What am I supposed to do now?" I encouraged the mom to hold her ground, respect her daughter's opinion, but keep her eye on the ball. The ability to write an essay and make a formal speech doesn't make her mature, but it does make her a good candidate for the debate club.

If your teen pushes back because he bought the game with his money, consider reimbursing him. Some parents sell the game system and use the money to purchase new hobby items.

You can choose to make this a "win-win" situation. Your kids are allowed to protest, but you must move on. Set a time limit on the conversation. Remember what a coach would do. Lay out the game plan but don't keep hashing it over. Then go have some fun.

You will need that support system. After the first wave of reactions from the initial announcement, frustration may ramp up again. Your young child will be happy to spend more time with you. Your not-too-addicted preteen may get past the initial shock after a few weeks. But your middle schooler or early high schooler may take six weeks or more to adjust.

Depending on the severity of the screen addiction, you may need a professional counselor to help get you through this communication phase. How do you know? If your child is demonstrating anger or getting violent, or you're afraid to talk to your child, consider engaging a counselor.

GO COLD TURKEY

"You have to go cold turkey. Nothing will compare to the excitement and draw of the game. And you need to absolutely get it out of your house. Otherwise, the kids will find it. I know. I did."

—Adam Brooker, former gamer

Recently, while waiting at a doctor's office, I met a mom who was very vocal about the video game obsession of her boys. She told her friend that she got so mad that she took the console out on the driveway and beat it to pieces with a baseball bat. "It was the best feeling ever!" she said.

While I don't necessarily recommend taking a bat to your screens, I have to admit that it would feel pretty good! Having a calm and organized plan around removing the video games, tablets, and smartphones works much better. This is the cold-turkey approach. Or, as Dr. Victoria Dunckley says, "You need to take an all-or-nothing approach because of the way the brain is wired. It's really the only way this is going to be successful. Once the nervous system become overstimulated you have to remove all unnatural stimulation for it to reset."[1]

THE CLEAN SWEEP

✓   **Take all screens out of your kids' bedrooms.** This includes gaming consoles, old smartphones, Chromebooks, e-readers, laptops, TVs, etc. Even if the device is not "activated," your child can still get online via WiFi.

✓   **Remove all old screens from the rest of your house.** Search for old devices, computers, game device and phones in unused desk drawers, closets, and even the attic.

✓   **Locate all device chargers.** By removing extra chargers, you remove the ability for them to charge up a secret "borrowed" device.

✓   **Remove the merchandise.** It's time to retire the *Minecraft* bedding, game-related magazines, game posters, and T-shirts. Change the environment.

✓   **Remove the devices from your house.** It's best if you can store the devices you are removing off-campus. Don't just hide them in your house. Remember how you were able to find things that your parents hid—like Christmas presents—when you were growing up? When the devices are out of the house, it's easier for everyone to stick to the plan.

Now, go collect *all* the devices, so we can get to the fun part!

TIP: One mom was beginning these steps and realized she needed to take away the smartphone from her 12-year-old daughter. After talking to her daughter about the decision, her daughter asked for a coffee shop gift card as a trade for her phone so she could hang out with her friends a few times a month. What a great trade! Deep down her daughter knew that spending time with her friends was what she really wanted. Other ideas include trading devices for season tickets to ball games, theatre performances, or other local events.

TIP: The other point to consider—if you think your child is mature enough to manage smartphones and video games, keep in mind that you have no control over her peers. She will be exposed to every bit of content that her most immature peer brings to the virtual platform. What this means is that you must decide if they are ready for that exposure and factor that into your screen plan. Like secondhand smoke, the effects may be hard to spot, but they're dangerous, nonetheless.

STEP FIVE: REBUILD LIFE SKILLS

"A young adult lacking life skills is not prepared to succeed in life...having things done for you leads to 'learned helplessness.'"
—Julie Lythcott-Haims, *How to Raise an Adult: Break Free of the Overparenting Trap and Prepare Your Kid for Success*

LIFE SKILLS ARE FUNDAMENTAL skills that need to be learned, built, and practiced in childhood and adolescence. The lack of life skill development hurts your child's future potential in most every area of his life, from job success to, most importantly, relationship success.

Screen overuse replaces opportunities to build life skills during the best window of time to establish these cornerstone habits. Finding more comfort in the virtual world, your kids easily get stuck in a cycle of dependency on you for basic daily living tasks. It's difficult to get a screen-dependent kid off the game or phone long enough to do chores around the house. And he's not getting any help from his brain that's wired to conserve energy, and crave low-effort, high-reward activities rather than work. The lack of motivation in this area will cause family conflict and is an example of how screens can drive a wedge between you and your child.

The stakes are high. Screens not only distract your kids from learning and practicing life skills, but they can also affect the quality of the work being done. If screens are lurking in the background as an optional activity, your child will have a hard time focusing on doing a good job. Work will be just good enough to allow him to get back to his screen. You will get exhausted managing it and resentment will build. Your child will view you as the bad guy who is keeping him away from his first love.

LIFE SKILLS MATTER MORE THAN YOU THINK

Think of your home as a life skills workshop. Here are a few reasons why you should make practicing life skills a priority for your kids:

- o You want them to be independent and move out of the house one day.
- o You want them to be competent, happy, and successful in a career and a meaningful relationship one day.
- o You want them to understand the good feeling of purpose and accomplishment, and not just be spectators in life.
- o They must learn that life is not like living in a hotel, and you are tired of doing the laundry, while they play *Fortnite* or take selfies on the couch.

o   Practicing life skills and chores is the best way
    to develop self-discipline.
o   You are running out of time.

You are not looking for perfection, but you do want them to
become independent and experience the connection between
effort and reward. As your child begins to own her successes and
find pride in the accomplishment of hard work, she will become
more balanced. You are encouraging deliberate practice for the
things that matter most before she engages in more screen time.
You are living the dilemma: every hour spent on non-
productive screen entertainment takes time out of more
important skills. Striking a balance is very difficult.

In addition, when you bring basic life skills back into your
child's life, you get the added benefit of getting him to practice
soft skills—emotional skills—such as communication, empathy,
work ethic, interpersonal skills, leadership, time management,
teamwork, and attention to detail. These skills are difficult to
learn for someone who spends most of his time on a screen.

LIFE SKILLS CHECKLIST

The following is a short (clearly not all-encompassing) list of
what your child is capable of:

- ✓ Making her bed
- ✓ Cleaning the kitchen
- ✓ Cleaning bathroom
- ✓ Taking care of pets
- ✓ Making school lunches
- ✓ Waking up on his own

- ✓ Doing own laundry
- ✓ Cooking a full meal
- ✓ Mowing the lawn
- ✓ Organizing and cleaning garage
- ✓ Managing money
- ✓ Maintaining his own schedule and appointments

BUILD GRIT IN YOUR CHILD

"Highly self-disciplined adolescents outperformed their more impulsive peers on every academic-performance variable," says Charles Duhigg in his book *The Power of Habit*. "Self-discipline predicted academic performance more robustly than did IQ. Self-discipline also predicted which students would improve their grades over the course of the school year, whereas IQ did not....Self-discipline has a bigger effect on academic performance than does intellectual talent."[1]

In her book, *Grit*, Angela Duckworth says that grit is passion and perseverance for long-term and meaningful goals.[2] It matters because research shows that grit is an essential component of success, more so than talent or IQ. In other words, if our goal is to develop healthy, well-adjusted adults who can succeed in life, then our goal is to raise gritty kids. That means teaching them that self-discipline, hard work, and effort matter.

While a screen can be a tool for some information gathering and typing essays, your child will not develop real grit in the midst of his *Call of Duty* game or while browsing Instagram. No matter how hard you stretch the *screens are good for my child* defense, at this point in his life, your child's entertainment screen time will never transfer to building life skills or developing a work ethic. These valuable skills are only built through personal experiences offline. Solving a problem in a video game doesn't help you learn how to solve a real-life problem like fixing your broken bike, organizing the garage, or being late for school.

So what does he need to develop grit and overcome a screen addiction at the same time? Chores. A lawn mower, a broom, or a sink full of dirty dishes is a good place to start.

The Harvard Grant Study, a 75-year longitudinal study measuring success and happiness at the end of life, reveals that warm relationships and doing chores as a child are two of the best predictors of future success.[3] While life is fun and full of rewards, it's also challenging and requires us to do hard things. Your kids will win in life by being gritty and getting comfortable with doing hard things. Your job as a coach includes helping your kids by giving them a lifelong gift of developing a strong work ethic.

Learning to do chores is more than getting by with a lick and a promise so you can get back to your video game or Instagram. It includes organization: planning ahead for the task, gathering supplies, and finishing the job. It also includes keeping track of schedules, such as when the trash truck comes or when certain regular maintenance is due on the car or lawn. It's not about doing the laundry once and checking that off the list. It's about adding and building the routines into your child's lifestyle.

Infuse as much purpose and responsibility as you can find in all your day-to-day living, and don't shy away from having your kids do dirty work. Everything you need to get your kids on track is right under your own roof. When kids start developing life skills and contributing to the family in this manner, there's not a lot of time to waste on meaningless screen activities.

THE BIG ANSWER

By now you may be wondering when a good time is to allow games and phones. The beauty of being a ScreenStrong Family is that the answer to that question is suddenly very easy! When are your players ready for the next level? When are they ready for a smartphone or the privilege of hours of gaming? When they demonstrate that they are competent and mature. For example, when your child gets a job and buys her own phone plan.

Based on their life skill development, your teens will show you when they are ready for more screen time. The answer will become crystal clear. If your teens still need you to remind them to brush their teeth, do the dishes, wash their own clothes, and quit gossiping about their friends, they are certainly not ready for a life of leisure playing video games nor can they be trusted to be mature on social media. It's not their fault; they simply aren't ready yet. Don't make this harder than it needs to be. A good coach never puts his player in the game before he's ready. Make a list of life skills and determine when your children will be able to balance screen time based on how accomplished they are with real life.

"Parents are all too worried that their children will be misfits if they are not plugged in. We should be far more concerned with helping our children realize their potential as human beings. The blindness around this digital technology is much like a blindness around the phenomena of peer orientation. What is normal is judged by what is typical, not by what is natural or what is healthy. This blindness has been exacerbated by our love affair with technology in the naive assumption that what is good for adults must also be good for children."

—Gordon Neufeld, PhD, and Gabor Maté, MD,
Hold on to Your Kids: Why Parents Need to Matter More Than Peers

TIP: Stop doing chores for your kids. I have heard many excuses about why parents don't assign chores to their kids, such as, "They don't do it as well as I expect;" or "Their job is school; therefore, I feel that my job is cleaning." "He's an athlete and doesn't have time." "It's not worth the arguments." These are all dangerous excuses. Not only will you send an unprepared child out into the world (if he ever actually leaves your house), but you are also doing a disservice by not allowing him to build confidence and maturity that come with the experience of a job well done.

STEP SIX:
REPLACE SCREEN TIME

"...interests are not discovered through introspection. Instead, interests are triggered by interactions with the outside world. The process of interest discovery can be messy, serendipitous, and inefficient. This is because you can't really predict with certainty what will capture your attention and what won't... Without experimenting, you can't figure out which interests will stick, and which won't."

—Angela Duckworth, PhD,
Grit: The Power of Passion and Perseverance

THINK OF ALL THE TIME your child currently spends in front of a screen. It's frightening, right? Now imagine what your child's life would be like if you converted mindless screen hours to developing real interests. Let's take a look.

Let's say that between sixth and 12th grade, your child spends two hours a day on gaming or social media (noneducational screen time). That's a total of 5,110 hours before she graduates from high school. Bump that to four hours a day on a screen, and it's 10,220 hours.

What could your child do with an additional 10,220 hours?

A lot.

Perhaps she would become a pianist or an artist, start a small business, or make the school tennis team. Perhaps he would be better at baseball, take the lead in the school play, get a job, have more time with family, or just have more time to read and think. Bill Gates used some of his hours to read the entire *World Book Encyclopedia* during his teens. Thank goodness he wasn't spending his hours playing *Grand Theft Auto* or gathering likes on Instagram! My son Adam often says that he wishes he had his 10,000 hours back. That's his estimate of the time he wasted on gaming. He enjoyed piano and tennis, but never developed those hobbies.

When you practice piano and tennis you get better, but when you practice a bad habit (or a potentially addictive behavior like social media) for hours a day, you get worse. You become addicted. Consider a balanced ScreenStrong lifestyle to be perhaps the best and biggest gift you will ever give your child. It will give her more time to develop a variety of interests. Managing this time resource well is the gift with a great return on investment!

DISCOVER NEW INTERESTS

Can your child find something to do on his own? Can she fill an afternoon without her phone? Can he invent a game in the backyard or organize a group for Frisbee golf? They may not know exactly where to start. Retraining is required. It will be difficult to foster and grow new interests at first because nothing else is as easy and stimulating as a screen for a child's brain. You have your job cut out for you. As their coach, your most strategic job right now will be to help your children find non-screen activities, even if they protest. And they will.

Many parents report that their kids have no other talents and that's why they got hooked on their screens to begin with. They explain that sports are "not his thing," or "she isn't gifted at music or art." Or even, "They are gifted at screens instead." But all kids are "gifted" at screens because of how screens are designed. It's like saying, "My child's talent includes eating donuts!"

But research says that we need to not be concerned with natural gifts that much. According to Duckworth, "As much as talent counts, effort counts twice."[1] Few children are born "gifted." The majority of us need to work hard over time to develop an interest or skill. Even truly talented kids work relentlessly at their skill. We assume they have it easier somehow. But could being talented or gifted actually mean that one has an overabundance of grit? Do they work so hard at a skill that they look gifted to others? Perhaps if your child practiced piano for over an hour every day, he would look gifted, too.

PLAYING IS HARD WORK

The first two to six weeks of trying to develop new interests will be difficult depending on the level of your child's screen dependency and age. Some kids are happy with replacement activities while others take longer to come to terms with the anger and rebellion over not having their device.

In the beginning, you may need to organize regular social gatherings, investigate club opportunities, or simply be present by sitting and reading a book while he practices piano in the living room. Your children are not just replacing the screen activity; they are replacing a relationship void and may feel lonely without the company of the device. Find some friends to join them on a sports team or art class. Eventually they won't need you to direct them as much. Do not grow weary. Through discovering other interests your children will begin to heal and grow again. You will need to be strong, involved, and, most importantly, keep a positive attitude. You can't just throw them in the pool and expect them to swim right away.

HOW TO FIND THE RIGHT ACTIVITIES

The key to your child developing interests is for you to open the door to many activities. It begins with having fun and engaging in unstructured play followed by meeting others who do the same activities. When we combine the idea of building relationships with building interests, we strike gold. When friends share the same activity, your child becomes motivated to continue. He begins to get better at the skill and the shared activity becomes more fun. He gets more confident and begins to feel that he has a talent and is motivated to continue. But this takes time. Surround your family with other families who share the same interests.

Interests are generally discovered through non-stressful play activities that are enjoyed over and over again. For example, my daughter discovered her love for gymnastics by hanging from trees in the backyard. We didn't know that she would grow up to be a college gymnast, and neither did she at the time. It all started with opening the door—literally—and spending a lot of time in the backyard. I took note of her interest and got a trampoline, then I signed her up for gymnastics lessons. If she had been glued to a screen upstairs in her room, her story would be dramatically different.

Many parents, including me with my oldest, allow our kids to decide all their interests. We give them choices. My son chose video games. But kids are not mature enough to know what's good for them so they will typically pick the easiest thing. While you certainly want to start with their interests, many screen-dependent kids have lost all interest in non-screen hobbies, so they need extra help discovering some new activities. Guiding them as a coach often means helping to structure their likes.

Many kids need strong direction, especially through middle school. The nature of a preadolescent brain will cause them to be fickle with how they spend their time and what they like. Peer politics also exert significant influence over their desires. If all their peers trade existing hobbies and activities for video games and social media, which is common in middle school, your child will think they need to do the same thing. As they get older, they can have more say, but they still need you to as a stabilizing force in guiding their activities. Stay strong and stand firm.

Screen-replacement activities should be a mix of unstructured things to do anytime (outdoor activities, reading, freeplay, board games, social gatherings, cooking, etc.) and structured activities (sports teams, music lessons, art lessons, dance, drama, etc.). As their coach, you will guide your children toward multiple choices from each of these two categories. Your mission is to help your child find at least five other activities and hobbies that interest him outside of his screens.[2] Here is a short list of activity ideas to help you get started. Think of something from each category.

Movement: sports, exercise, dance
Creativity and imagination: art, cooking, writing, theatre
Social activities: board game nights with friends, scouts, parties, church groups
Music: lessons, garage band, tickets to symphony, plays
Reading: reading time with family, magazine subscriptions, book clubs, library time

REDISCOVER EXTRACURRICULAR ACTIVITIES

Will being in the school play or serving on the yearbook committee help your child be more successful in his career one day? Research says yes. Studies show that kids who are involved with extracurricular activities fare better in many measurable metrics: higher self-esteem, better behavior, better grades, and better life success. The key is in the practice and follow-through, as opposed to dabbling, especially when things get tough.[3] Screen activity is not an extracurricular activity. Extracurricular activities meet on a regular basis (generally after school), include a group of same-age peers, and are, most importantly, led by committed adults. This means an adult (coach or mentor) is providing good examples, teaching character, building relationships, and helping to develop other life skills through the activity. The coach may encourage practice on a regular basis, require discipline, or focus on a specific goal. The benefits of extracurricular activities are rooted in the elements of commitment, follow-through, grit, and, most importantly, character building with the help of a caring adult.

Teaching your kids to first show up, and then follow through with an activity is more important than the activity itself. How committed they are to the school newspaper will transfer to the boardroom one day. It really has nothing to do with winning an award in school and being the best; rather it's about the experience and not quitting. It's all about building grit through the commitment. Studies indicate that kids who stick to at least two extracurricular activities for at least two years in high school do better in life.[4]

RE-ESTABLISH REAL PLAY

"The ability to play is critical not only to being happy, but also to sustaining social relationships and being a creative, innovative person," writes Stuart Brown, MD, in his book, *Play: How it Shapes the Brain, Opens the Imagination, and Invigorates the Soul.* According to Brown, a rich play history is the best gift you can give your child.[5] A profound biological process play actually creates new connections in the brain and then strengthens them. It's critical to play throughout our whole life. Without play, numerous executive functions may not mature properly. Real play reduces stress, sharpens social skills, and teaches adaptability.[6] It's necessary for children to learn and practice in-person problem-solving skills in a safe environment. Real play is practice for life.

Isn't my son *playing* on his video game? Brown says no. "When someone is domineering, aggressive, or violent they are not engaged in true play no matter what they are doing," He continues, "When someone is gaming or watching a screen, there is no engagement in the natural world, no development of the social nuances that are part of maturation in us as social species."[7]

Young children naturally know how to play, but kids who have developed a screen addiction have lost this skill. They expect the screen to do the work and entertain them and have forgotten how to entertain themselves. For this reason, parents must put unstructured real play back in their kids' lives. For older kids and teens, it'll be a harder task because their brains have been conditioned to seek out instant screen entertainment. They may have missed many chances to take part in this part of innovative play, but you can help them recapture it.

Your kids are never too old to play. I'm reminded how my boys and even their older teen friends still love the big disk tree swing we have in our backyard. They are taller than I am now, but they still love to play outside, and that's a good thing. We all need more real play in our lives.

RARELY LET THEM QUIT

"The coach is mean, and no one likes me."
"My friends are on another team."
"It's too hot and my cleats hurt!"

Every child feels like quitting sometime, but this is especially prevalent in screen-saturated kids. Remember that hobbies take time to develop. One sports season or six months of music lessons is not enough time. Developing interests requires sticking to something hard over a long time. Quitting is easy and so is playing video games. If a video game isn't going well, then your child learns to simply restart, reset, reboot, or just pull the plug and start over. If a social media issue isn't going well, she learns to simply delete, unlike, unfriend, or alienate others at the push of a button. A pattern of giving up begins which later leads to missed opportunities.

Because kids don't know what's good for them when it comes to hard work and getting out of their comfort zone, they need you to be their coach and help them stay in the game. That means not letting them easily quit activities. You keep your eye on the end goal even when he's having a meltdown on the kitchen floor because he doesn't want to go to basketball practice, or she has made a 10-point argument about why she wants to quit volleyball.

Consider the following tips regarding quitting activities:

- Never ever let them quit midseason, even if they are hurt and it means they are only sitting on the bench.

- Beware of middle school. This is the age when apathy can take over and is the time when most quitting occurs. Plus, your teen is a master salesman at this age and you are getting worn down. Quitting the football team to spend more time playing *Madden NFL* is not a good idea.

- Don't allow them to quit immediately after a low point. Allow them to discuss stopping an activity only after they have had their best game or season, or at least after some time has passed and you have had time to help them work through a challenging season.

This isn't about being a harsh parent but being a savvy coach and setting a high bar. Have an upbeat attitude and don't get on your teen's roller coaster. A respected coach once told me when my middle school daughter was in a brief quitting spell with her sport: "Mom, do not get wrapped up in her teen emotions (her drama). Fix *your* attitude. You smile and you be happy, and the rest will work itself out." That was some of the best parenting advice I ever received.

In a few pages I have tried to encourage you to restructure your kids' likes, and I know this is a hard step. It takes tough love. But this step is key to reversing your child's screen obsession. Be warned, there will be complaining, and this will be a hard thing for you to overcome. But you have developed enough grit and follow-through over your lifetime to drive a complaining child to an activity he doesn't like. You know that he needs to work through it, and you are going to be there to focus on the end goal when he can't and help him do just that.

Our middle school boys were getting in the bad habit of complaining about a certain activity every time we took them. It happened to be their least favorite activity, but one that we felt was good for them. My husband and I were worn down over the complaining so we decided to try something. I explained to them that complaining was not allowed on our family team. I decided not to assume that they knew that rule. They could voice their opinion, and we would set a time for that discussion, but the constant complaining every time we got in the car would have to stop. The coaching worked. To our surprise, they stopped complaining. Is it always that easy?

Sometimes it is.

TIP: Your child should get a job. She should begin to pursue ideas for a job on her own. Young kids can get little jobs around the neighborhood. At age 14, your child can get a job outside the house. At 16 there is no excuse. Will you have to drive her to her job? Maybe. But that's a small price to pay for extra help in building grit, character, and hard work in your child's life.

STEP SEVEN: RECONNECT YOUR FAMILY

"The fundamental issue we as parents need to face is that of the competing attachments that have seduced our children away from our loving care...Today's children are not only turning to their peers but they are actively and energetically turning away from their parents."
—Gordon Neufeld, PhD, and Gabor Maté, MD, *Hold on to Your Kids: Why Parents Need to Matter More Than Peers*

ATTACHMENT AND BELONGING ARE a child's most powerful drives. This means that strengthening your child's connection with his family should be one of your highest priorities as a parent. Don't be swayed by the culture that says that games, phones, and friends are more important to a child than his parents or his family.

Your child will have a primary attachment and compass. It'll either be you or her peers. If she chooses peers, the attachment will transfer to her screens because screens represent her peer world. The more your child is on video games and social media, the greater the peer influence will be.

You will see that even though peer attachments are superficial, your child will hold on to them with a death grip and defend them because a teen's biggest fear is being alone. With blind allegiance, your child will follow her lost peers anywhere. The kids end up raising each other, like the blind leading the blind.[1]

Gordon Neufeld and Gabor Maté do a wonderful job of explaining this loss of direction in their book *Hold On To Your Kids: Why Parents Need to Matter More Than Peers.* When a child becomes primarily peer-oriented instead of parent-oriented, parents increasingly lose their ability to guide and influence their child and, even worse, can become the object of disrespect and ridicule. When this happens the child also starts to lose their natural shield of protection against stress: parent attachment.[2] Your child's peers will never adequately satisfy his need for attachment. Only his family can do that. However, he will keep trying to make his screens fill that need and the roots of screen addiction take hold.

Kids of all ages need warm and caring relationships with responsive adults more than they need peer influences. As surprising as it may sound, even older teens thrive best within strong, closely knit families. The benefits of raising parent-oriented children are many: less drug and alcohol abuse, fewer suicide attempts, less violent behavior, less early sexual behavior, less stress, and better emotional health.[3]

While peers become increasingly important in a child's development, it's never okay for your child's peers to replace your role in his life. You, not his peers, must remain the dominant influence as your child's personality and identity develop.

Helping your kids stay attached to your family team is your most important parenting job. You have everything you need for this job: unconditional acceptance of your child. Peers don't come close to being able to fill that need for your child.

STRONG FAMILY RELATIONSHIPS

We saw earlier that our brains are shaped by our environment, and the most important elements in a child's environment are his relationships. Our survival depends on human attachment. It's true; we live longer when we invest in warm, in-person, lasting relationships.[4] For every hour we spend on our screens, traditional face-to-face interaction time with other people drops by nearly 30 minutes.[5]

Strong family relationships also protect the brain. As Susan Pinker, PhD, says in her book *The Village Effect*, our relationships are just as important as what we eat and how much exercise we get—actually more important. Not just any social contact—but real time face-to-face contact. "Our social ties influence our satisfaction with life, our cognitive skills, and how resistant we are to infections and chronic disease....Dozens of recent studies demonstrates how close social contact affects our physiological resilience, that's how briskly our body bounces back after trauma—MRIs show greater tissue repair."[6]

STRONG FAMILY CULTURE

Every team and every family have a culture. Culture is defined as the beliefs, shared goals, values, and attitudes of a group. It's the group's identity. Your culture is like your brand. It incorporates the decisions you make, what you value, how you parent, and how you are perceived by others. Even if you have never focused on purposefully promoting a specific family culture, your family already has one—and your kids know exactly what it is by how you live your life.

If your kids do most of their living in a gaming or social media world, they will pick up the values of that culture. You know this is happening when you feel that your child never comes home. You notice that they stop sharing with you the things that matter. They stop asking questions about life. Because the screen world is so captivating, when left unchecked, it gradually takes the place of your family culture. The longer this is allowed to continue, the harder it'll be to reverse. Social conformity can easily become a stronger force than our own values if we don't anchor our kids in a vibrant family culture.

Your child's screen culture is fighting hard for his attention and allegiance every day. So our family culture must be deeper and stronger. Your son's brain craves the efficiency of just going with the flow in his video game, and it takes a lot of effort for your daughter to resist what the group around her is doing. For better or worse, the way their group does things becomes the way they do things.

Teens aren't the only ones influenced by peers; parents are, too. Our own desire for social acceptance can allow the culture to become a surrogate coach for our family's screen decisions, rules, and values if we allow it. We can easily follow the lead of other parents, letting them influence our decisions. It's hard to go against the crowd when it comes to decisions about what age to get our child a phone or what video games should be allowed. We are susceptible to peer pressure, too. Just like teenagers, we care too deeply about the opinions of others, and fail to follow our own instincts, reasoning, and common sense.

How can we strengthen our own family culture, while we still participate in the larger screen-influenced culture? First, we must determine what our family values are. Second, we must communicate them to our kids relentlessly. Third, we must never allow the screen culture to become primary—it must *always* remain secondary to our family culture, and only be used as a tool to reinforce our values, not as a babysitter that only pulls our kids away from them. When we consider a ScreenStrong lifestyle and don't use the internet as our primary source of entertainment and downtime, we are on our way to building a stronger family culture.

As the coach, it's your privilege to strengthen your family culture. What do you want your family to be known for? Pick three or four character qualities that rise to the top of your list. Does your child's screen time develop this core value well? Will more time on a game or social media help get your kids closer to developing their talents and adopting your values?

Here are *some* examples of values that might define your family:

Honesty: We never lie to each other.
Grit: We never give up. Even when it's hard.
Faith: We know there is a higher power that we answer to.
Humor: We don't take ourselves too seriously.
Listen: We make eye contact and patiently listen to others.
Creativity: We make it ourselves.
Humility: We take the high road; we don't criticize others.
Fun: We make family fun a priority with our time.
Extra-Mile: We go above and beyond. We exceed expectations.
Compassion: We care for those around us.
Morality: We have a porn-free home.
Respect: We show respect to our elders.

Once you identify core values most important to your family, write them down and display them in a prominent place so everyone on the team is reminded of what you value most. Be sure to talk about these values often instead of assuming your kids know them. This will bind your team together. Beyond having a strong set of shared values, here are some other elements of a connected family that you should consider strengthening:

Time

Kids need in-person time with you. If possible, spend at least 15 minutes a day with each child if possible, then more as a family. One study shows that the average family spends only 14 percent of their time at home together. The rest of the time is spent alone engaging in screen activities.[7]

Touch

A child who is deprived of touch exhibits anxiety, fear, and difficulty in adapting to any new environment or situation. Babies who are not touched enough are anxious and agitated. Children who are not touched enough can't learn.[8] Make time for purposeful hugs every day for every child, including your teens.

Talk

It's common for parents to tell me that once the video games and phones are gone, they notice that their kids talk much more to them. It helps to eat regular meals together and have purposeful conversations.

Laughter and rough-housing

Laugh together and include rough-and-tumble play for all the kids. These things keep you connected with your child.

Play and movement

Make exercise a priority. Take walks after dinner, participate in physical activity after school, or do simple workouts together at home if possible.

Downtime

Your child should have alone time every day. You may have to schedule this. Downtime must be protected much like the quiet nap time that we scheduled when they were little. Screen time is not downtime.

Hard work

Everyone has responsibility around the house. "Everyone helps" should be the rule.

WIN THEM BACK

When you feel like your kids have checked out from your family, you fight hard to get them back. You realize how important this is, you roll up your sleeves, and you go to work. Why is it so hard to get your kids off the screens and back as active participants on your family team? Because old habits die hard. Depending on how long they have been gone, the re-entry into family life may be rocky at first, especially for the older teens who have been checked out longer. Reattaching is hard emotional work.

What's the good news? The odds are in your favor. Your kids really want to belong with you even if they don't act like it. They want you to be their hero. They want to be like you. They even brag about you to their friends when you are not around. They are watching you and they want to learn from you. We learn best from the people with whom we are most attached. And the bonus is that when you get your kids back, you will have more fun with them.

How do you want your kids to remember their childhood? Will they have fond memories of all the hours they spent on Snapchat and hours spent playing *Fortnite* in a little corner of the house? Or will they feel like they were connected to their family with a bank of family stories and memories to carry them the rest of their lives? Stories of caring for beloved pets, camping in the backyard, beating Dad in driveway basketball games, playing board games with siblings, or being on a championship sports team? These are the moments that need to be deliberately worked into our new game plan. The great thing is that you get to decide how this plays out. You are their coach and you get to determine what this season called childhood is likely to be remembered for.

TIP: Ask your kids to write down 15 things that make your family special. This will give you some insights on what makes them feel connected to your family. Keep doing this!

CONCLUSION

"We have allowed kids to be guided by same age peers (via games and phones) rather than insisting on the primacy of guidance from adults. As a result, American kids now grow up to be less imaginative, less adaptive, and less creative than they could be."
—Leonard Sax, MD, PhD, *The Collapse of Parenting*

CONGRATULATIONS, YOU MADE IT!

When I was raising Adam, I was completely unprepared for my new role as the Game Cop Mom in our home. I was exhausted and so confused. But we figured it out, and I'm so happy to be able to share our story so that you don't feel like the only one suffering through the endless screen battles in your house.

If your kids are obsessed with their screens, they need to be rescued from their virtual worlds. Now. By you. Your children need *you* to help minimize the stress in their lives and guide them to reach their highest potential. Move childhood back outside. Get them off their video games and smartphones so they can develop life skills and relationships. Don't be afraid to go against the digital culture and stay strong.

Much has been covered in this little book. I hope you see the ScreenStrong lifestyle is much easier to manage than trying to manage the constant frustration of mindless screens.

Deep down your child is begging for you to coach him and understanding the brain science makes your job much easier. Leave the paralyzing emotion and indecision behind, and take a stand for your kids. Rethink how screens help, or hurt, your child's development. Then hit the pause button on screen habits that are stealing your family's joy. Most of all, realize the seriousness of family attachment and the short time you have left to influence your kids.

In your new role as coach, you will be more confident, less stressed, and happier with your new game plan. Your family will be healthier. Your kids will also be less stressed and happier as you make it possible for them to discover many new talents. Your family connection will be stronger.

You won't get much help from the culture at large, but you will get help from like-minded families when you start your ScreenStrong small group. You will change your home environment and welcome your child back to your family team. You will be amazed when your child develops new life skills. You will start to enjoy your child again and look forward to spending time together. I have a feeling you will never return to the screen-dominated, chaotic life that once defined your home.

This is not a scrimmage; this is the championship game that you will win. You may not feel prepared for the task at hand, but you have everything you need for this job. You will not be perfect; no one is. You will have doubts when your child starts to get angry, but don't give in. One thing is true: you will never give up seeking the best path for your child.

When your kids reach the college years, they'll be balanced and prepared. They'll bring with them the life skills and values that you taught them and the self-control they practiced. Your family stories, shared experiences, and memories will make them strong. They won't suddenly binge on screens because they have practiced a lifestyle that provides rewards better than a screen. They'll want to fill their lives with what matters most: time spent making memories with people.

You have given them the gift of belonging and, most important of all, they will belong to your family. You will know in your heart that you did the right thing. Like all of us who have taken the bold step to be ScreenStrong—instead of screen-obsessed—you will never look back.

"Adolescence is not a problem to be solved. It is an experience to be lived. At the end of the adventure, when your adolescent is an adult, you'll be able to answer the question of whodunit: you and your kid, together. From there, to paraphrase Dr. Seuss, they'll have places to go and fun to be done. Thanks to your help, the game can be won."

—David Walsh, PhD, *Why Do They Act that Way? A Survival Guide to the Adolescent Brain for You and Your Teen*

ScreenStrong provides real solutions to prevent and reverse childhood screen addictions. Using medical science as our guide, we provide a fresh approach that helps parents regain direction and confidence as they face one of today's most crucial parenting challenges: raising kids in a digital world.

Do you need a plan to reduce screen time, but don't know where to start? Our ScreenStrong Challenge is a week-long break from video games and smartphones. It's designed to give your kids an opportunity to experience the things they've missed out on since gaming and social media stole their free time. It's a chance to step back, recharge, and reconnect with each other as a family.

Visit www.ScreenStrong.com for more information.

APPENDIX 1

DIAGNOSTIC CRITERIA FOR VIDEO GAME DEPENDENCY

Diagnostic criteria by Douglas Gentile, PhD, Iowa State University:

1) Over time, have you been spending much more time playing video games, learning about video game playing, or planning the next opportunity to play?

2) Do you need to spend more time and money on video games in order to feel the same amount of excitement as other activities in your life?

3) Have you tried to play video games for shorter durations of times but have been unsuccessful?

4) Do you become restless or irritable when you attempt to cut down or stop playing video games?

5) Have you played video games as a way to escape problems or negative feelings?

6) Have you lied to family or friends about how much you play video games?

7) Have you ever stolen a video game from a store or a friend, or stolen money to buy a video game?

8) Do you sometimes skip household chores in order to play more video games?

9) Do you sometimes skip homework or work in order to play more video games?

10) Have you ever done poorly on a school assignment, test, or work assignment because you have spent so much time playing video games?

11) Have you ever needed friends or family to give you extra money because you've spent too much of your own money on video games, software, or game Internet fees?

If you answered "yes" to six or more of these questions, then you most likely have an addiction to video games. If "yes" is answered to five or fewer questions, then there may be a problem. Behaviors become "addictions" when they disrupt real life, such as school or work performance, real life relationships, and activities of daily living. Use this survey as a guide to determine if video games and/or internet use may be a problem in your life, but do not use the survey to make a "clinical diagnosis."

SCREEN IMMERSION (GAMING) LEVELS

Screen immersion gaming levels by Families Managing Media. After working with families for years, we have found the following levels to be accurate. While they fit a gamer profile, they can apply to smartphones and social media screen use, too. The screen addiction begins because your child develops a relationship with his screen, just as he would with a girl. While it may start as a causal relationship, the persuasive design that's being built into gaming platforms can tempt your son until he's fully drawn into a "fatal attraction" relationship with his game. Here is a summary of the progression:

1) **Just Friends, a.k.a. the Casual Gamer**
   o   Plays a few times a month.
   o   Demonstrates that he's emotionally and socially balanced.
   o   Maintains many relationships with family and friends.
   o   Has many hobbies.
   o   Communicates well.
   o   Shows no game-related behavioral changes.

2) **Going Steady, a.k.a. the At-Risk Gamer**
   o   Plays at least once a week.
   o   Loves the game but isn't obsessed; can easily be drawn back into other activities.
   o   Talks about gaming on a regular basis.
   o   Still has plenty of friends who like to participate in non-tech activities.
   o   Begins gaming more than he used to.

3) **Risky Affair, a.k.a. the Dependent Gamer**
   - Plays two to three times a week or occasionally binges.
   - Thinks and talks about gaming episodes a lot.
   - Has some angry outbursts with gaming disappointments.
   - Begins to drop out of other activities or friendships.
   - Starts to show signs of narcissism.
   - Parents have a gut feeling that he's headed down the wrong path.
   - Becomes harder to manage time limits at home.

4) **"Fatal Attraction," a.k.a. the Addicted Gamer**
   - Plays every day.
   - Develops anger issues, temper, and narcissism.
   - Changes in daily living: sleep issues, poor eating, personal hygiene, grades, etc.
   - Has few outside activities or non-gaming friends.
   - Has signs of withdrawals when he's forced off the game.
   - Displays antisocial behavior: verbal abuse, hurting siblings when they interrupt his game play, disrespecting parents over game rules, online bullying, lying, destroying family property (throwing controllers), cheating, etc.
   - Detaches from parents and family relationships.

APPENDIX 2

THE ADOLESCENT BRAIN COGNITIVE DEVELOPMENT (ABCD) STUDY

This is the largest long-term study of brain development and child health in the United States. This 300-million-dollar study is gathering information about teen brains. They are following 11,874 kids (nine-10-year-olds) for 10 years.

The preliminary results are groundbreaking, the first cohort of data with 4,500 kids includes two findings:

1. **Premature thinning of the cortex.** The first round of MRI tests with kids who are on their screens over 7 hours a day (including school screens) reveals premature thinning of the cortex. The area in the brain responsible for processing the information our five senses gather from real-world experiences. When a child is on a screen, he's not experiencing the real world. Since the brain begins to prune away connections that are not being used, this area of the brain is prematurely thinning out. Normally we see this thinning in older teens and adults not nine-10-year-olds. The cortex also is responsible for executive functioning—i.e., higher order thinking, such as data consolidation, problem-solving, and planning. It also helps us regulate our responses to emotions that come from deeper areas of the brain. ABCD researchers found that this thinning in the cortex was correlated with lower crystalized intelligence (knowledge gained from

living life, such as vocabulary as opposed to fluid intelligence.)

2. **Lower scores on thinking (cognitive) and language tests.** In the group that spends more than two hours a day on screens, early results have shown lower scores on thinking and language tests.

Sources: National Institutes of Health, ABCD Study, ABC 60 Minutes 12/9/18

ENDNOTES

INTRODUCTION

1. Jean M. Twenge, Thomas E. Joiner, Megan L. Rogers, and Gabrielle N. Martin. "Increases in Depressive Symptoms, Suicide-Related Outcomes, and Suicide Rates Among U.S. Adolescents After 2010 and Links to Increased New Media Screen Time." *SAGE Journals*, Association for Psychological Science. (Nov. 14, 2017.) Also see Twenge interview on CBS *60 Minutes*: "Ground Breaking Study Examines Effects of Screen Time on Kids." In this program, *60 Minutes* goes inside a landmark government study of young minds to see if phones, tablets and other screens are impacting adolescent brain development.
2. Review Myth blog post: Stop Believing These 10 Screen Myths, found on Families Managing Media
3. Catherine Sebastian et al, "Social Brain Development in the affective consequences of ostracism in adolescence, Brandon cognition 7 to 2010.
4. "Learning, Social Technology, and Healthy Behaviors." Linda Charmaraman, PhD, and Jennifer Grossman, PhD. https://www.newton.k12.ma.us/cms/lib/MA01907692/Centricity/Domain/1262/Bigelow%20Panel%20Discussion.September%202018%2001%2001.pdf
5. #Being 13: Inside the Secret World of Teens, CNN Special Report. (video)
6. TEDx Talk on YouTube: Quit Social Media by Cal Newport
7. "Silicon Valley parents are raising their kids tech free— and it should be a red flag." *Business Insider.* https://www.businessinsider.com/silicon-valley-parents-raising-their-kids-tech-free-red-flag-2018-2
8. Leonard Sax, MD, PhD, *The Collapse of Parenting: How We Hurt Our Kids When We Treat Them Like Grown-Ups.* (New York: Basic Books, 2016.) Sax explains the notion of forbidden fruit: "The research strongly suggests that if you instill habits of good behavior and self-control in our son or daughter throughout childhood and adolescence, then you have improved the odds that your child will continue to do the right thing after leaving home." If you

are raising a gamer or if your daughter is spending hours a night on her social media, "then the odds are not very likely good that when they arrive at college they will say, 'My peers are spending much time on social media sites and playing video games, but I will nevertheless turn over a new leaf and become a more virtuous person.' That's not very likely." 132-133.

9. Sax, *The Collapse of Parenting*, 132.
10. *Will Your Gamer Survive College?* By Melanie Hempe
11. *Can Your Teen Survive—and Thrive—Without a Smartphone?* By Melanie Hempe

THE BRAIN SCIENCE
1. Frances E. Jensen, MD, with Amy Ellis Nutt. *The Teenage Brain: A Neuroscientist's Survival Guide to Raising Adolescents and Young Adults*. (New York: Collins, 2016), 28.
2. Gary Small and Gigi Vorgan. *IBrain: Surviving the Technological Alteration of the Modern Mind*. (Harper, 2009), 32.
3. Jenson, *The Teenage Brain*, 77.
4. Pinker, Susan. *The Village Effect: How Face-to-Face Contact Can Make Us Healthier and Happier*. (Vintage Canada, 2015), 8.
5. "Exercise Is ADHD Medication." *The* Atlantic, www.theatlantic.com/health/archive/2014/09/exercise seems-to-be-beneficial-to-children/380844/
6. Stuart Brown, MD, *Play. How it Shapes the Brain, Opens the Imagination, and Invigorates the Soul*. (New York: Avery, 2010.) Chapter 7, Does Play Have a Darkside, 178.
7. Victoria L. Dunckley, MD. *Reset Your Child's Brain: a Four Week Plan To End Meltdowns, Raise Grades, and Boost Social Skills by Reversing the Effects of Electronic Screen-Time*. (Novato, CA: New World Library, 2015), 41.
8. Jensen, *The Teenage Brain*, 89.
9. Small and Vorgan, *iBrain*, 48.
10. Andrew P. Doan, MD. *Hooked on Games: The Lure and Cost of Video Games and Internet Addiction*. (Coralville, IA: F.E.P. International, Inc., 2012),
11. Dunckley, *Reset Your Child's Brain*, 12
12. Twenge, Jean M. iGen: *Why Today's Super-connected Kids Are Growing Up Less Rebellious, More Tolerant, Less Happy—and Completely Unprepared for Adulthood (and What This*

Means for the Rest of Us). First Atria books hardcover edition. New York, NY: Atria Books, 2017. Print.

13. Dunckley, *Reset Your Child's Brain,* Chapter 2.
14. Douglas Gentile. "Pathological Video-Game Use Among Youth Ages 8 to 18." Psychol Sci. 2009 Jun;20(6):785.

STEP ONE: BECOME A COACH

1. Angela A. Duckworth, PhD, *Grit: The Power of Passion and Perseverance.* (New York, NY, US: Scribner/Simon & Schuster, 2016), 212.
    Duckworth, page 213, There is really no need to study this anymore. For the past 40 years "Study after carefully designed study has found that the children of psychologically wise parents (authoritative parenting) they are better than children raised in any other kind of household." In one study of 10,000 American teenagers, regardless of gender, ethnicity, social class, or parent's marital status, teens with warm, respectful, and demanding parents learned higher grades in school, or more self-reliant, suffered from less anxiety and depression, and we're less likely to engage in delinquent Behavior. The same pattern replicates in nearly every nation that's been studied and at every stage of child development."

2. Authoritative parenting:
    Authoritative parenting revisited: History and current status. Baumrind, D. (2013). Authoritative parenting revisited: History and current status. In R. E. Larzelere, A. S. Morris, & A. W. Harrist (Eds.), *Authoritative parenting: Synthesizing nurturance and discipline for optimal child development* (pp. 11-34). Washington, DC, US: American Psychological Association. https://psycnet.apa.org/record/2012-15622-002

    Parent styles associated with children's self-regulation and competence in school. Grolnick, W. S., & Ryan, R. M. (1989). Parent styles associated with children's self-regulation and competence in school. *Journal of Educational Psychology, 81*(2), 43-154, https://psycnet.apa.org/record/1989-34682-001

STEP TWO: GATHER SUPPORT

1. Screen Strong small group information can be found on ScreenStrong.com (by Families Managing Media)
2. Joe Clement and Matt Miles. *Screen-Schooled: Two Veteran Teachers Expose How Technology Overuse Is Making Our Kids Dumber.* (Chicago: Chicago Review Press Incorporated, 2018). This book is a good resource for working with screens in a school setting.
3. Book recommendations for a Screen Strong book club include:
    o   *How to Reset Your Child's Brain* by Victoria Dunckley, MD
    o   *Disconnected* by Thomas Kersting, PhD
    o   *The Wired Child* by Richard Freed, PhD
    o   *Hooked on Games* by Andrew Doan, MD, PhD
    o   *Screen Schooled* by Matt Miles and Joe Clement
    o   *The Big Disconnect* by Catherine Steiner Adair. EdD. This is a good book for parents with all age kids but especially the younger age group.

STEP THREE: PREPARE FOR CHANGE

1. Charles Duhigg, *The Power of Habit: Why we do what we do in life and business.* (New York Random House, 2012). 19.

STEP FOUR: REMOVE THE SCREENS

1. Dunckley, Chapter 1.
2. Dunckley, 230-232
3. World Health Organization. September 2018. "What is gaming disorder? Gaming disorder is defined in the 11th Revision of the International Classification of Diseases (ICD-11) as a pattern of gaming behavior ("digital-gaming" or "video-gaming") characterized by impaired control over gaming, increasing priority given to gaming over other activities to the extent that gaming takes precedence over other interests and daily activities, and continuation or escalation of gaming despite the occurrence of negative consequences. For gaming disorder to be diagnosed, the behavior pattern must be of sufficient severity to result in significant impairment in personal, family,

social, educational, occupational or other important areas of functioning and would normally have been evident for at least 12 months. https://www.who.int/features/qa/gaming-disorder/en/

STEP FIVE: REBUILD LIFE SKILLS

1. Charles Duhigg. *The Power of Habit: Why We Do What We Do in Life and Business.* (New York: Random House, 2012), 131.
2. Angela A. Duckworth, *Grit, p.* 258
3. The Harvard Grant Study: spanning 75 years and counting--from 1938 to the present, researchers identified two things that people need in order to be happy and successful: The first? Love. The second? Work ethic. https://www2.bostonglobe.com/lifestyle/2015/12/08/rese arch-indicates-sparing-chores-spoils-children-and-their-future-selves/ZLvMznpC5btmHtNRXXhNFJ/story.html

STEP SIX: REPLACE SCREEN TIME

1. Duckworth, *Grit,* 35.
2. Cris Rowan. "Disrupting the Progression from Early Screen Use to Screen Addiction." Children's Screen Time Action Network, https://screentimenetwork.org/resource/disrupting-progression-early-screen-use-screen-addiction
3. Duckworth, *Grit,* 225.
4. Duckworth, *Grit,* 234-236, 317
   Study Adolescents' participation in organized activities and developmental success 2 and 8 years after high school: do sponsorship, duration, and intensity matter? https://www.ncbi.nlm.nih.gov/pubmed/18473646
5. Brown, *Play,* 26.
6. Brown, *Play,* 33-34.
7. Brown, *Play,* 183

STEP SEVEN: RECONNECT YOUR FAMILY

1. Gordon Neufeld, PhD, and Gabor Maté, MD. *Hold on to Your Kids: Why Parents Need to Matter More Than Peers,* (Vermilion, 2019), 26-27
2. Neufeld and Maté, *Hold on to Your Kids,* 99-100.
3. Neufeld and Maté, *Hold on to Your Kids,* 103.

4. Pinker, *The Village Effect*, 9.
5. Nie NH, Hillygus DS. *The impact of Internet use on sociability: Time-diary findings*. IT & Society. 2002;1:1–20. [Google Scholar]
6. Pinker, *The Village Effect*, 9.
7. Rao TS, Indla V, Reddy IR. *Is digital boom spelling cerebral doom?*. Indian J Psychiatry. 2012;54(4):301–303. doi:10.4103/0019-5545.104790
8. Rowan, *Disrupting the Progression*, 116.

ABOUT THE AUTHOR

Melanie Hempe is the Founder and President of Families Managing Media, a national nonprofit organization that offers a countercultural approach to eliminating childhood screen dependency. Through its flagship ScreenStrong initiative and the 7-day ScreenStrong Challenge, FMM empowers parents to pause or delay the most addictive types of screen use by their kids, while emphasizing the importance of developing life skills.

Through her many speaking engagements at local workshops and conferences around the country, Melanie brings together her compelling personal story and her command of the emerging research on childhood screen addiction to provide practical solutions to struggling families. Her work has been featured in local and national media including *Psychology Today, Thrive-Global, The Wall Street Journal, NPR,* and *CBS.*

Melanie holds a Bachelor of Science in Nursing from Emory University and is the author of three books. She lives in North Carolina with her husband and their four children.

Made in United States
Orlando, FL
28 May 2025

61647360R00060